Shiny Side Up

Up

A humorous look at teaching your child to drive

By John E. Larkin, Ed.S.

State of Florida Commercial
Driving School Instructor

Definition:

Shiny Side Up – returning the Driver's Ed car to school with the tires still in contact with the pavement. (A mostly routine occurrence)

Dedication:

To my wife Elizabeth (Beth) who humors me like only the best wife could.

"You want to do what??!!!"

"Really"?

"Uh, ok." "Just be careful."

I'm being careful honey, I promise.

To all my fellow Driver's Ed instructors– Bill, Richard, Betty, Ken, Carlos, Jerry ,Ron, Scott, Mark and Greg; my fellow teachers who were always looking for ways to make Driver's Education better, safer and more fun for the kids. You guys are the best! This wouldn't have been nearly as much fun without you.

 Keep bringing 'er in "shiny side up".

Table of Contents

1   Note to Parents

2   How to Use This Book

3   How to Talk to Your Teen about Driving

4   Choosing the Car to Use

5   Equipment You Will Need

6   Does that Tire Look Low to You?

7   Getting Ready to Drive

8   Where to Go that's Safe

9   Drill 'em So the Other Drivers Don't Kill 'em

10 The Rules of the Road

11 Don't Even Think about Yelling

12 Don't Feed the Bears

13 Driven to Distraction

14 The Power of Prayer

15 Deadly Errors

16 Driver's Ed and Students with Disabilities

17 Troubleshooting Driving Problems

1.   Note to Parents

Many parents teach their child to drive. Lots of those parents will also send their child to a driving class to hone their skills and in some cases reduce the cost of their auto insurance. If you are a parent reading this before teaching your child to drive, good for you! You've at least considered that someone ought to teach your child to drive before throwing them to the wolves on the road. Congratulations for being a good parent. You're already brighter than a large percentage of parents in the U.S. and we're only 6 sentences into the book. Way to go!

Look, you as parent are the first and best teacher of your child in all things. As a paid teacher, I am very good at what I do, but you have more impact in your child's life than I ever will. This book is designed to help you keep making that positive impact, and keep your child happy and safe on the road.

Teaching your child to drive is one of those stepping stone events in life that help prepare your child for responsible adulthood. Let's be honest, it's a point of pride for you. You get to tell those horror stories to all your friends at parties for the rest of your life, and you get a child who loves and looks up to you. What's better than that?

Seriously, this is one of those events that help to transition children to adulthood. It's a major responsibility step in a child's life to get a driver's license and begins the transformation of that snotty, know-it-all 15 year old you birthed to a young adult of whom you're proud.

From one parent to another your proudest moment as a parent is when they're grown and gone and call home and ask "hey Dad, what do you think about __" because they trust you. You're in a transformational period in your child's life. This crazy, anxious event Driver's Ed is one of those things that gets you to the responsible adult child you love. Please don't kill your child now; you'll miss out on the good part.

As a parent, I taught both of my own children to drive. This is well before I had my Driver's Education training and was getting paid to teach other people's children. While our travels were somewhat hair-raising (as yours will be too) in the end I can't remember any individual harrowing experience, which is normally a good sign.

As it turns out both of my daughters became good drivers. As they were learning to drive we often had them ride together; the new driver in the driver's seat and the passenger in charge of navigation, radio, air conditioner and cell phone. It was not, as my neighbor suggested, trying to kill them both at the same time. It just worked out that way occasionally.

Yes, we had a couple close calls. Our oldest child had only been driving on her own a very short time when she put her car backwards through a cattle fence after discovering "Black Ice".

We were visiting with my in-laws who were staying at a resort close to our home when our daughters had to leave to go home to finish homework. About 5 minutes after they left we got a call from our passenger daughter, who very calmly told us that they had wrecked the car. She was just fine. Our other daughter, the driver, was hysterical and the worst part for us as parents was to hear her wailing from the other seat as daughter number two made the call.

Five minutes down the road they had run into a misting rain, on a newly paved road and discovered the wild ride we call 'Florida Black Ice". Black Ice is when a road releases some of its oil in the afternoon heat, and then with the addition of just a tiny bit of water, becomes as slick as ice until the rain washes the oiliness away. You can tell students about this, but unless you have access to a professional skid pad somewhere you really can't teach dealing with it.

To make a long story short both daughters were fine, the car was fine and all we had to do is extricate the car from a bit of old cattle fencing alongside a former pasture.

As a parent of teens, you get somewhat used to the fact that all of your warnings and all of your knowledge is looked at like so much rubbish. Every so often something manages to sink in (without great expense or injury) that makes your kids say "hey, I guess the old man did know what he was talking about." Don't ya just love it when that happens?

2. How to Use This Book

As an experienced driving instructor I make a lot of corrections on the fly as I am conducting a Driver's Ed class. This is hard won knowledge, gained through teaching a large number of students and comparing notes with fellow instructors, over a period of years.

Or in student language, "been there, done that, got the T-shirt".

I would hope I don't have to write "**DON'T BUY THIS BOOK AND READ IT WHILE DRIVING!**" But there is a reason for the sticker on your blow dryer warning you not to use it in the shower.

"They" are out there; you've probably met them.

Promise me that you'll read the book, cover to cover, **in a chair, not behind or adjacent to a steering wheel**.

I've included as many of my tips and techniques, and as much of the verbiage I use with the kids as I can remember. There is also a section in the back that will help you to correct many of the errors common to new drivers. If you know these ahead of time they will help to take a lot of the hair-pulling (yours) and gnashing of teeth out of the process. Your heartburn, ulcer, high blood pressure or migraine condition will appreciate your preparation, I promise.

In the end you are out there on your own, it's your judgment, your call, and your neck on the line. Big boy rules apply here (more on that in a moment). I've tried to include as much safety related material in this guide as I could. I'm not liable for any decisions you make while trying anything I've done or suggested. You are an adult now, you are responsible for yourself. Please take it slowly, be careful and have fun.

3.   How to Talk to Your Teen about Driving

Before you allow a teenager anywhere near a car you need to have a sit-down discussion with them about what it means to be responsible in the car. In the South we call this a "come to Jesus meeting", which is especially appropriate here as we'd both like to keep your child alive.

Let's be honest, you're about to turn a child loose in a ton and a half of steel and hard plastic that has a annual kill rate approaching that of Phillip Morris'. Ok so I'm exaggerating a bit, but you get the idea. Cars can be dangerous, even fatal. You need to have a discussion about what you expect while your student is behind the wheel.

Big Boy/Big Girl Rules

Here are the discussion points you might want to cover:

If you get a ticket you are responsible to pay that ticket.

 In our state, parking in a handicapped spot is about $200, speeding in a school zone or road work zone is double the ticket cost (so probably starts about $225 and goes north from there very quickly)   I'd say a month or so without the car would also be sufficient to help reinforce the lesson that **speeding is entirely voluntary thus can be controlled by the driver 100 percent.** No excuses.

If you hurt someone; you are responsible.

 In Florida if you hit a road worker you go to jail, you hit a kid at a bus stop and the parents get to kill you on the spot. Hey, it's the South and "some people just need killing" is statute law in most states down here.

If y*ou wreck the car you get to pay to fix it (and bum rides until it's fixed).*

Personally, I have a $1000 deductible on my policy and just the thought of paying the first grand keeps my own driving in check.

Don't even think about touching your phone while you're driving.

I'll check, so I'll know. Don't do it. If you have to return my call (and only I'm that important), pull over and call me back. If I ever catch you texting and driving you're done for good in my cars (or on my insurance).

Let the passengers control the radio and or the temperature controls.

As a novice driver you don't need to be doing that while you're driving.

Eating, in the car?

That's why McDonalds has tables inside. Use them.

The car is not your bathroom.

You will not brush your hair, put on your makeup, brush your teeth or shave any part of yourself (feel free to Google "woman driving while shaving bikini area"-no disgusting pictures, just a funny story that will make you wonder if you really want your kids to drive, ever.)

Feel free to add your own ideas here.

4.   Choosing the Car to Use

When teaching Driver's Education at school we have
several nice cars purchased for our use. Those cars have
an automatic transmission, and power equipment to
make it easier for new (and varied size) drivers to get
fitted into the car. We also have a foot brake on the front
floorboard of the passenger side for the (frequent) use of
the instructor.

If you have any of those options on your car or cars at
home (and you've even installed a foot brake on the
passenger side for driving with your wife/husband) by all
means, drive that car. If for some reason don't own a car
with a second brake, try to pick the most appropriate car
for teaching your child to drive.

A car with the emergency brake in the center console (a
hand brake) is ideal, gives you something to help you slow
the car down if necessary. **Note: the parking brake will
"lock" the back wheels causing a skid if applied too
quickly – if using to slow the car, apply gradually.** If your
car does not have one of those just take slower steps
before leaving the parking lot.

Have mercy on your new driver; maybe don't start with
the car with manual transmission.

If your choice is between the old pickup truck, or the new
AMG appointed 7 series BMW, if you could afford the

BMW in the first place you ought to be smart enough to have them use the pickup. We'll scale everything to size to work with the larger car anyway. More on that in a little bit.

There is nothing wrong with letting your child know how good they have it learning to drive in whatever car you presently own.

As we're practicing, often I like to turn the motor off then switch the ignition back to on (while parked in a safe spot) and challenge the kids the turn the steering wheel. I learned to drive in an old pickup with manual steering, manual brakes and a "three-on-the-tree" manual transmission on the column. It does make kids more appreciative if they know what things use to be like, especially when they are not the ones paying for the car.

Author's note on choosing that all important "First Car" for your child:

Gentlemen, if you are buying a car for your darling daughter, who is a new driver, don't go out and buy her the car of her dreams if you haven't gotten one for your wife first. Unless of course you are trying to get rid of your wife. Let's be honest, your wife probably deserves the car more than your daughter and your daughter cannot possibly appreciate what it took to make it appear in the driveway. Your wife on the other hand may very well appreciate your gesture, and maybe more than once.

When you finally do allow your child to get that first car, rather than buying your child a new convertible, get them a hand me down from some aged relative or neighbor. I always suggest an "old lady car". Buicks, Pontiacs, Cadillacs, Oldsmobiles, something slow moving, decidedly "unsporty" and safe. Until a child is old enough to buy their own car they should own something homely enough to have a name like "Roger".

Roger is our trusty 15-year old Camry with about 160,000 miles. Roger is old, ugly, slow and reliable as a car can be made (please don't tell Roger we said those things). Named by Daughter Number One (the cattle-fence killer) below is a picture of "Roger". My daughter somehow took a picture that made the car look nice. Maybe I should Craigslist it now.

5. Equipment You Will Need

Every time before we begin a new class we get the students together and let them know there are several things that are required for Driver's Education class.

Here's the list:

Your state issued license and insurance paperwork.

Closed toed shoes. In the South most of the students have any number of pairs of "flip-flops" which they wear to school because it's nice and warm most of the year. Flip flops and sandals have a bad habit of getting caught in the pedals and causing some tense moments while driving. Have your student wear a pair of tennis shoes or other closed toed shoe that have some feel for the pedals. Steel toed work boots may also not be a good option as they have no feel for the pedals. Hey folks, I don't dictate teen fashion, just observe it.

Sunglasses. We require all of our students to bring a pair of sunglasses. After school as the sun is setting, the glare is intense. The kids need a decent pair of glasses to be able to see especially near sunrise or sunset. Occasionally students will give me a bit of flack on this point saying that glasses are distracting or they don't have a pair or don't like them or whatever. In that case, I routinely direct them by a roadside memorial for a local teen killed while driving into the morning sun. Maybe sunglasses would have allowed her to see the oncoming truck, maybe not. But the outcome may have been much different. Remember, you can ignore reality; you cannot however ignore the consequences of ignoring reality.

School appropriate clothes. It is distracting to the driver if he or she is always tugging at their clothes to cover up in the air conditioning, or adjusting something that doesn't fit well. Wear something comfortable, covering and not a distraction to you or to other drivers.

Believe it or not, I have in my driving career, passed a **family** in a car driving around town buck naked. They're out there somewhere folks. Be careful.

6. Does that Tire Look Low to You?

Chances are that the teen you are preparing to teach to drive has no idea about any of the parts of the car, or how to check to make sure the car is generally safe to drive.

Here's a quick tip – **YA GOTTA TEACH 'EM THAT TOO!!!**

Walk your student around the car, have a look at the tires. Are they full of air? (check), do they have tread on them?(check), are there any strange bumps or things sticking out of them?, no (check). Nothing falling off the car/flapping in the breeze (check).

How to open up the fuel door. This seems really simple until you realize that every auto maker has their own special way to get that door open and sometimes even 3 or 4 ways depending on the model from that manufacturer. For example, GM just started using a new push-in latch like a cabinet door.

I've seen three grown men walk around a car for 20 minutes trying to figure out how to get the fuel door open, only to have one of the students finally figure it out. I know because one of the men was me. If you don't want a late night call from the gas station, figure it out ahead of time.

Open up the hood. Teach them how to check the fluid levels; brake, battery, power steering, coolant/antifreeze, oil and transmission fluid. The engine you save may be your own.

7.   Getting Ready to Drive

Seats

Before anybody starts the car, take the time to get the driver "fitted" in the driver's seat. If your car is like many new cars you have 3-5 levers or buttons that make the driver's seat do things even your mother wouldn't do for you.

Have your student sit down in the driver's seat with the door open. Stand next to them in the doorway and help them to see all of the controls used to manipulate the seat. Spend a bit of time fitting the seat to the driver. Make sure the driver can see over the dash, is close enough to be able to fully depress the gas pedal, without having to stretch.

You will want to make sure they are close enough to grip the steering wheel at the 10 o'clock and 2 o'clock positions (like we were taught) with a bit of bend in the arms.

Steering wheel

Many of the newer manufactured cars have a tilt wheel steering featured buried in the bottom of the steering column. Once you find the lever (you knew about that, right?) show them how to tilt and or telescope the steering wheel into a comfortable position for them. Try to get the wheel at about an 80 or 90 percent extension of the arms while the driver is sitting back comfortably in the seat.

To test fit, the driver's hands should be able to hang by the wrist over the steering wheel. If that works, they are properly adjusted.

Note: New cars as of the last 18-20 years have an airbag inside the steering wheel. Airbags are propelled with an explosive charge.

Many new drivers are inclined to hug the steering wheel to feel in control. You might repeat the words "explosives" and "rhinoplasty" a couple times and that should decrease the desire to hug the steering wheel.

Mirrors

While you're still standing there, show your student where the controls are on the door or the dash for the mirrors (if you have power mirrors). Now close the door and get in on the passenger side. Have your student adjust the side mirrors such that they can see following cars behind our car, with just a little bit of the side of the car showing in the mirror. This helps to eliminate blind spots.

Now ask them to adjust the rear view mirror. Most newer cars have a prismatic rearview mirror. Show them how to flip that little lever in the back for night driving.

Controls

Go over all of the controls on the steering column and dashboard with your student. They have no idea how to turn the high beams off and on, use the intermittent wiper function or use the turn signals.

Dashboard lights and gauges

Explain briefly the need to check for any strange lights on the dashboard. If you turn the key to the on position before starting the car, most models display all of the lights on the dash. If your car has gauges instead of lights, take a little time and explain what reasonable readings are for all of the gauges.

Years ago I worked in the automobile business. Every so often we would have a young person bring their car in to the service department with the little oil light shining brightly on the dash and the car either running poorly, or not running at all.

The conversation usually went like this:

Customer: "My car's not running right; I don't know what's wrong with it."

Service Tech: "Sounds really bad, did you check the oil?"

Customer: "...check the oil?"

Service Tech: " The engine oil. That light that's shining on the dash."

Customer: "...that's what that is?"

Service Tech: "You might want to call home for some money; this is going to be really expensive"

Remember, the engine you save may be your own.

Air conditioner and radio

Explain how to use the climate controls for the car, especially the defroster/defogger functions to keep a clear windshield or rear window.

As far as the radio, you've probably been asking them to set the clock and radio presets on the car since you bought it anyway. Make sure you've got the radio set the way you want – **then turn it off for today**.

Seatbelts

The proper answer to any question about having to wear seat belts is always the same: always, every time, regardless of where you're going, when you're driving, what you're driving, how long you're driving or how safe you may feel.

I have personally pulled two conscious, but dazed people out of burning cars in two different accidents. Both cars had rolled over in the accident. Both people when I got to them were sitting upright, on the ceiling inside of their **burning**, rolled over car. Both were very conscious, neither was coherent. Both cars ended up total losses, both drivers ended up safe by sheer dumb luck and the grace of God.

Both drivers were incoherent because of the "washing machine" effect a rolling car has on a loose item in the car, like an unbelted driver.

As ridiculous as it may seem, in the second accident the driver was driving down a dirt road, all alone save the Driver's Ed car I was in with my students. You see, I used the dirt road to teach novice drivers because it's so safe and you don't have to deal with a lot of pressure from other drivers. Some days we would drive down the road and never see another soul.

On this particular day I had just finished instructing my student driver to slow down into the turns and stay on his side because sometimes "stupid people come flying through the turns sliding sideways because they're going way too fast. Sometimes they even over correct once or twice and they just roll the car over". From the other direction the little Honda SUV did just that, rolled over a time or two and caught fire right in front of us upside down.

Folks, that's what we in the education business call a *"teachable moment"*.

8.   Where to Go That's Safe

In my area we are blessed to be in close proximity to city and country driving.

We are in a bedroom community surrounding a large metro area. Also within about 10 miles is rural farmland, with 2 lane roads stretching out for miles. All of this means a variety of driving experiences for the new driver, and safe situations as you gradually build up the new drivers' skills and self-confidence.

As you are preparing to teach your student to drive, you need to be on the lookout for a couple different driving areas (situations) that will help you to hone their skills.

Strip malls

I have several favorite spots I use for different situations/skill building. We have a couple unfinished strip malls in the area that are great for driving. One, fortuitously, looks like a ¼ mile drag strip with a cul-de-sac at the end. Great for high speed stopping drills, 3 point turns and parallel parking. I'll explain these drills in the next chapter. Another of the strip centers is a series of choppy parking spots surrounding building lots, ideal for teaching pedal control, turning and parking.

Subdivisions

Partially built out neighborhoods are great resources. One I use nearby has a roundabout built into the center of the development (forgot about those didn't you?). Quieter, built out subdivisions are also useful in teaching steering, turning and brake control at low speeds. Just be extremely watchful of the kids and the dogs.

Dirt roads

If you have any dirt/gravel roads nearby that you expect your student to ever have to deal with, you need to do some driving out there. A car handles much differently on dirt than it does on pavement. We have several dirt roads nearby, a couple of which transition back and forth between dirt, gravel, and pavement. All of them are remote and perfect for teaching the new driver.

Country roads

We are fortunate to have a number of long open roads winding out into the country just ideal for new drivers to learn at speed without the traffic pressure and multi-tasking requirements of the city.

City driving without construction

As I write this it seems like all of the roads in Central Florida are under construction.   City driving is harrowing for a new driver; pick some portion of the city around your area without construction to teach your new driver. I don't know how they do construction where you are from, but down here we alternate lanes. We cannot close roads altogether because we just don't have enough roads to go around. What that means to drivers is that in the morning the driving lane may be the right lane. By the time the afternoon rolls around the right lane may not be open at all and your path is completely different. Add in some dump trucks, earth movers and a handful of guys in orange vests and you're just asking for it sending a new driver through that mess.

Snow and Ice

Thank God we don't have snow and ice in Florida to deal with. We wreck our cars down here when it looks like rain. If you have to deal with snow and ice in your area find someplace very remote and extra safe before teaching driving under those conditions.

Refer to Chapter 14 regarding prayer. Good luck.

9. Drill 'em so the Other Drivers don't Kill 'em

If you ever learned to play a sport or an instrument, chances are your coach had you do some drills before you actually tried to play a game or the music.

Driving is similar in that aspect. You cannot put a teen out on a public road without teaching them pedal control, steering and some appreciation of where the car is in terms of objects and other cars. The following are drills that I do with the students to make sure they are ready for the road, before we get out on the road.

Low speed Figure 8's

This is often the first drill I do with new drivers, and anyone who has not had enough experience with pedal control and steering /proximity to objects. Go find an empty parking lot with a couple curbed "islands" in it that are in close proximity to one another. Have your student drive figure 8's around the island very, very slowly at first. This gives them an appreciation of how touchy the gas pedal and or brake might be and gives them some experience with steering the car around objects. If you do not have a strong stomach you're gonna love this (not!).

I once did this drill while we had a new instructor on a ride along with us in the back seat. After about three minutes the new instructor was in the back seat screaming "Oh Jesus help me". "Stop the car!" "Stop the car!!!" Really, you're gonna love this.

Have your student do figure 8's faster and closer to the island as they get more comfortable with the gas, brake and steering. Once you and they start to get dizzy, switch and do the drill the opposite direction for a little while. If it gets to be too much, stop, get out, and stretch for a while.

Ask your student to repeat until they can drive around the island, closely at a good speed and in a controlled fashion about 10 times in a row.

Gas pedal only Figure 8's

This is the second step once your driver is proficient at low speed. Have them use only the gas pedal, lightly feathering it to gain a bit of speed in the straightaway, learn to understand that turning will bleed off **some** of the accumulated speed. This is a low-speed drill to teach safe handling of the car, pedal control, steering and distance to objects.

Again, repeat until they can drive around the island, closely at a good speed and in a controlled fashion about 10 times in a row.

The Slalom Course

You can set up a slalom course with just about any objects that won't be hurt by running over them. Make sure whatever you pick also won't damage the tires or the undercarriage because you're about to run over some "stuff" on purpose.

We are provided with a half-dozen orange traffic cones in each of our Driver's Education cars. If you don't happen to have a bunch of traffic cones lying around the house (and please don't go steal them from the roadside – they're out there for a purpose) maybe try Frisbees or stuffed animals (they've outgrown those things anyway). Find something you don't mind driving over, but can still tell when you've hit.

A slalom course is set up by picking a series of objects, spacing them a distance apart and then driving in and out in a continuous S pattern throughout the length of the course.

Set the course up in a remote parking lot. I space the cones 13 paces apart in a straight line. I'm 6'4" so your paces may vary.

If your driver is brand new add another pace. If they've been driving a bit and are getting cocky, shorten up the distance to humble them a might. This drill works equally as well for the absolute beginner as it does for the novice driver.

Have your child begin at low speed and under control, gently swerving back and forth between the cones. As they get better, allow them to go a bit faster. Note: the faster you go the greater the tendency to make larger and larger turns which will eventually take you outside the course.

Here's the secret to the drill: This is really a turning drill. The faster you go, the faster you have to turn. As the car comes even with each cone, look at the next cone to steer around it. Students have a tendency to look at each cone until it's behind the car, which doesn't allow them to judge what's coming up.

If a car is moving forward, you want to be anticipating what's coming up next. I'll often tell the students as we are going through this "turn, turn, turn, look at the next cone, other direction turn, turn turn."

Trust me, it sounds stupid now but it makes sense when you're in the car.

Safety here is paramount, make sure you are in an untraveled space and will have time alone to drill. By the way, just because you've set up your training area and it's patently obvious that you are training a new driver, don't imagine that some idiot won't come flying up next to you, or follow you through the slalom course at high speed. Trust me on this, and pay attention while you are drilling.

Have your student do this drill until he or she is comfortable moving through the course at a good speed and their speed does not carry them out of the course. Five times through the course cleanly should be sufficient.

After your child has gotten the hang of this drill, you need to get into the driver's seat and show them "how the pro's do it". Show off a little, it's a parent's prerogative and maybe they'll finally think, "wow, Mom's really good!"

The slalom course and figure 8's can be done backwards as well, once you work on driving backwards.

Quick Stops

The quick stop is designed to teach the students how to bring the car to a safe, straight stop as quickly as possible. This is best done in a remote parking lot; some place where you can get up to about 40 miles per hour. It's just as simple as it sounds. In a straight line, bring the car up to about 40 miles per hour, on your command the student will stop the car as quickly as possible in a straight line.

Do this a couple times until you are comfortable they can stop the car very quickly, in a controlled fashion.

Backing up

Backing a car is harder than it seems, if you are teaching somebody else how to do the backing.

People in general tend to get spatially disoriented quickly if they are facing forward and moving backward. So it is important that as your student learns to back up, they are oriented properly in the seat.

To back a car up, the driver should turn to the right in the driver's seat, place their right hand behind the passenger's seat and look out the back window. The left hand is used for controlling the steering wheel as we move backwards.

Initially, you will want to have the student back up in a straight line and not turn the wheel at all. Doing this allows them to understand that the car moves in a straight line unless they move the wheel in some fashion.

Fancy driving exercises, like reverse figure 8's, can be done once the student is comfortable behind the wheel with the car moving backwards.

Roundabout or traffic circle

The roundabout is a newer phenomenon to driving in the southern United States. (Let's face it, in the South we're still getting comfortable with seatbelts and those turn signal thingys)

The roundabout or traffic circle is a traffic control device put in an intersection to eliminate the need for a traffic light or stop sign. Traffic moves around a central circle, until they reach one of a number of possible exits as needed. The roundabout allows the orderly, continuous flow of traffic through the intersection in a safe manner (or that was the thought when they built them.)

To proceed safely through a roundabout your car yields to oncoming cars when entering the circle. Once in the circle the car proceeds in a counterclockwise path around the circle to the exit point needed and then signals to exit the circle at that point.

I have been told horror stories of multi-lane traffic circles in Europe, and places where you drive on the other side of the road. Not to worry, I am fairly sure we fought wars to prevent that sort of thing from happening here.

3 Point turns

Good news! New drivers easily become proficient at 3 point turns with just a little bit of practice. The most important part of the instruction in a 3 point turn is making sure the student never ever tries that turn other than on a visibly empty road. Trying a 3 point turn on a busy road in most places is punishable by high-speed collision.

To begin your turn, steer the car parallel to the right side of the road near as possible to the curb without touching it, and stop. Turn on left turn signal. Crank the steering wheel left until it stops. Slowly release the brake and coast to the other curb, while holding the wheel cranked to the stops. Close on the other curb without hitting it.

Stop. Crank the wheel all the way over in the opposite direction until it stops. Hold it tight and back up (using proper backing posture) to the opposite curve without hitting it.

Once you have backed up to the curb turn the wheel all the way over to the left, make your turn and move the car back into the right travel lane as appropriate.

If these instructions cannot be followed before a car would enter your turning space, do not try to execute a 3 point turn.

Parallel Parking

This is the most difficult of all of the driving skills we attempt with Driver's Education students. I frequently tell students that if they find a big enough parking spot to begin with, any mistakes they make while parking can be easily corrected, if they remain patient.

Teaching parallel parking, and writing about teaching parallel parking is somewhat difficult. I am going to give you a written description of how to set up a parallel parking spot, and then teach a parallel parking lesson. You may find it easier to have your student check out a couple videos online about how to do parallel parking before you begin.

I found several helpful videos online from YouTube and www.dmv.org (a free site, but not an official government site) that help give you a quick look at how do parallel parking with short videos.

Believe it or not, it's easier to do parallel parking with other cars around, so... if you can find a quiet spot to practice (meaning a spot without witnesses), with a car in front, or behind that often makes make it easier to start.

If you don't have that perfect spot you can make it with traffic cones or some other safe, soft, squishable object.

In your safe driving spot, set the objects up in a row in front of the parking space, perpendicular to the curb. Add another row, for the back of the parking space, 13 paces away, again perpendicular to the curb. Now you're standing there thinking, "This looks really big". (Look, I'm sure there is some place on earth where all of the parking spaces are the same size, politicians don't lie and taxes never go up, but I've never been there.) Use this spot for now, it is well sized for a standard 4 door sedan.

Before you do your parking I like to get the students out of the car and walk through what I want them to do in the car. It gets them in the motion that I want them to make without the burden of trying to steer right away.

Try this: Walk forward, past the empty spot in your imaginary car. Walk up to the point where the rear door or rear tire on the right side is adjacent to the cones (the back of the imaginary car in front of you). Put on your imaginary right turn signal; crank the imaginary steering wheel all the way to the right until the stop. Begin backing in at an angle. As your imaginary front wheels come even with the imaginary rear of the car in front of you begin opening up your imaginary steering wheel slowly. As you get into the parking space, continue opening your wheel as you slowly move your car backwards and parallel to the curb. As you reach the back of the parking space, and a position parallel to the curb, move forward evenly spacing yourself between the imaginary cars in front and behind you.

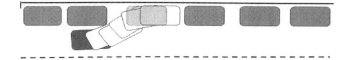

Daughter Number 2 sent us this lovely picture of herself parked in at college. That's her car, "Donkey" on the left. The other cars were inches from both the front and back bumper.

Try to leave yourself enough space to maneuver out of your spot later on by parking your car equidistant from the adjacent cars. Otherwise you may have to go back to the Library and study for a few more hours before you can leave.

10. The Rules of the Road

Depending on your state, your student has probably had at least some sort of written test on the rules of the road. So a basic understanding of the laws here is expected.

I've tried to include a lot of the things we talk about and have experienced during our driving classes.

Quick check: You're not reading this book in the passenger seat right? I didn't think so.

The Prime Directive

Probably the first rule you need to reinforce to your new driver before getting out on the road is this: **EVERYBODY OUT THERE IS *#&@ING NUTS AND MAY TRY TO KILL YOU WHEN YOU LEAST EXPECT IT.**

Not paying attention, for even an instant while driving may cost you. Once you convey that thought, and reinforce it with horror stories from your own experience, you're probably about ready to get out on the road.

Leaving the Parking Lot

If your state Department of Motor Vehicles is anything like my state Department of Motor Vehicles you can teach your child to drive well enough to pass the state test without ever entering a public road. (Embarrassing but true)

Now obviously that is not good enough for any sane individual. But it is, unfortunately, state law. So while you are driving around the parking lot, make a practice of requiring your student stop at the stop bars on the ground, signal, drive on their side of the traffic lane, and signal to pull into a parking space. It will get your student prepared to pass the test and builds good habits. Then you prepare them for reality on the roads.

The Monologue

One of the things I have found most helpful in working with beginning drivers is a running monologue to give constant instruction and or correction as we go. Since the radio is off, and any other students are quietly seated in the back of the car also listening to instruction, I have nothing competing for the student's attention with my instruction. Until the new driver is fairly competent on the road, this quiet, calm voice in their head is what keeps us safest while we drive. Once your driver is somewhat more competent, you can add a quiet radio in the background (maybe something they can't sing to initially) and then a discussion in the backseat.

Chapter 16 helps you to understand that the new driver cannot multi-task and why it is safer for all involved not to encourage them to share their attention initially.

Now imagine us leaving the faculty parking lot for a minute with the Driver's Ed car and I'll walk you through the beginning of the monologue.

"Ok, let's pull out slowly, watch for cars backing out into traffic. Right turn signal. Come to a complete stop at the stop bar. Nice tight turn take us out to the road. Pull into the left lane, we're going to make a left turn. Signal. Stop at the stop bar. Roll forward a bit so we can see around the fence, look both ways, pull out gently and let's go."

That's the beginning of a 3 hour Driver's Ed class. Now you may not have to do that with your child. Some students are extremely observant and pick up very quickly through watching what you have done. Some children are utterly oblivious and if you weren't putting food in front of them on a regular basis might actually starve in 3 weeks. You have kids, you know what I mean. Adjust accordingly.

With apologies to David Letterman; the Top 10 monologues.

The Stop Bar

That funny white painted line before all of the stop signs and traffic lights is ignored by most people and just confounds new drivers. First off they don't know what it is, can't figure out where it is, or how to get the car to stop nearly on it. By the way, the stop bar is positioned far enough back of the intersection so that you can be parked behind it and a turning truck with trailer will not casually glide **over** the hood of your car.

Here's your talk: "Ok, slow down before the stop bar, nice gentle braking, ok stop here. Good. Now roll up to the intersection (stop sign) so you can see. Look both ways, nice gentle gas let's go."

Turns and Cornering

New drivers all have a tendency to "bury" the car into a turn, that is, to run full speed at a turn, realize most of the way through it they're going way too fast and then panic and try to stop in a straight line (regardless of whether there is pavement in front of them or not). This can be an easy correct with your monologue:

"Ok slow down into the turn, coast (foot covering brake but not applying) through the turn, gas to get out of the turn." Lather, rinse and repeat. If you haven't said this about a hundred times to your new driver, you're not doing your job.

Intersection

"Ok, we have the right of way. As we roll into this intersection I need you to look both ways before we get into it. Anybody coming?" "Is that big truck able to stop?" "Coast up to it, accelerate through the intersection."

Turns

"We're going to make a left turn up here so put on your left turn signal and get into the left lane. Stop at the stop bar. As we're waiting for the light look and see where the median is. You are going to go around the median and stay in the near (left) lane. That will allow cars turning right to use the right lane. You do not have a left turn arrow so you have to yield to cars coming straight across. Ok, the light's green, look both ways, no one's coming let's go. Nice gentle acceleration, stay in your lane, good now up to speed."

"We're going to make a right turn at the intersection ahead so get into the right lane up ahead and put on your right signal. Stop at the stop bar. No cars are coming and we can do a right turn on red after stop. Look both ways and go ahead when it's clear. Nice tight turn, stay in your lane, ok bring it up to speed."

Merging

Merging is an unnatural act. Most competent drivers merge poorly. In Florida, the rule of thumb is if I've got less to live for, I get to go first (you understand that's sarcasm, right?).

So it is fun to teach your student to look in the direction of the merge, check for traffic in 360 degrees and make sure nobody is stopped dead on the ramp and everything is clear all while moving at what is probably a high rate of speed. Good luck on that.

"Ok we're coming up to a merge, you've got to make sure no one is coming as you're merging left into the traffic lane. Look in front of you to make sure no one is stopped on the ramp, look in your rear view mirror, check out where that car is, speed up to get in front (or slow down to let them go ahead). Keep your speed up and go ahead and merge. Gently turn into the other lane and keep going."

Passing

"We're going to pass the car in front of us. Since we'll be passing to the left, look in your left mirror and in your rear view mirror to make sure it's clear in the next lane. Next, give a quick look over your shoulder to make sure nobody got inside your blind spot. Now, gently accelerate and with an easy turn, pull out into the left lane. As we get in front of this guy, wait until you can see him in your rear view mirror and make sure he is still falling behind. Check your right mirror and give a quick look over your right shoulder. Continue gently accelerating and gently move back into the right lane."

Note: The look over the shoulder is actually difficult for students and the rookie driver will tend to try to turn around, while moving their hands (and the steering wheel) in the direction they are looking. Most are surprised to see themselves heading off the road as they complete this maneuver.

<u>As the instructors you need to watch the steering wheel as you give this instruction!</u>

Now I'm guessing if you're reading the book and instructing at the same time you've dropped the book, spilled your coffee and taught the kids some new words. Put the book down and focus – remember you promised!

Stopping to Park or Execute a 3 Point Turn

I always tell the students "your turn signal here is letting those people behind you know I'm getting ready to do something stupid". So to start the 3 Point Turn or stop to park say: "As you are coming up to the parking spot put on your right turn signal, that will let the drivers behind you know 'I'm getting ready to do something stupid' – like backing up in traffic (into that parking spot).

Now with a 3 point turn you are obviously (at least to you and me) not going to do this in traffic. Tell your students that while this is only for a clear, deserted road, you are signaling to let anyone who may come up on you quickly 'that you are doing something stupid' like turning around in the middle of the road. Your turn signal is the only indicator you have to let people know your intentions, use it liberally.

Normal Driving

Most of what you are doing would be considered normal driving. Normal driving is straight line, in some traffic and without serious challenges. The thing you want to watch for in normal driving conditions is that your student is paying so much attention to staying in the traffic lane and controlling the car they don't realize they are tailgating the car in front of them or running 5-10 miles an hour over or under the speed limit. You need to be commenting on all of those facts as they are driving under normal conditions.

"As we are moving along I need you to keep your pace behind the car in front of you, keep your pacing to the 2 second rule. Make sure you as you are driving you are scanning the road for traffic and obstacles, every so often look down at the speedometer for a ½ second and check your speed." If you are saying this every 30 seconds or so, for several hours, in just a couple weeks your driver will become accustomed to proper pacing and speed control.

Driving in the Rain

Driving in the rain is very similar to normal driving, but with more caution, less speed and more space.

Spread out your pacing to at least 3 seconds, slow down several miles per hour in driving, and begin slowing for your stops and turns sooner.

Make sure if it looks like rain before going out for a drive; reacquaint your student with the wiper controls and the headlights, including dealing with the high beams.

Instructor Note: In Florida we have a phenomenon called "Black Ice". Black Ice occurs when it has not rained for a time and the roads have accumulated a covering of oil as cars have passed by over time. As soon as it begins to lightly mist rain the oil mixes with the water on the surface of the roads and the road becomes exceptionally slick. Use extra caution at the beginning of a rain with following distance, speed and braking.

Driving in the Snow

Do you really have to go out in the snow? Really? Wouldn't a nice cup of hot chocolate be nice right now? Are you sure you want to do this?

If you really are sure you want to go out and drive in the snow, see all of the instructions for driving in the rain, and use exceptional caution. If the driving becomes dangerous please park and read the Chapter on Troubleshooting.

11. Don't Even Think About Yelling

So you're sitting there not reading this in the passenger seat you're wondering why in the world I would have a whole chapter about not yelling at your new driver. Here's why.

A majority of the students placed in my Driver's Ed classes are extremely nervous when they begin learning to drive. They are shaky, unskilled and clumsy at the controls. In a word, inexperienced. Many come to class after their parents or some other instructor gave up trying to teach them and ended up screaming at them when they got nervous.

In those cases I have two jobs to do. I have to teach them to drive and I have to calm them down enough to even try.

Typically, they will tell me after the first day or two, "You're so much easier to learn with because you don't yell at me."

What you Say is Important

As important as not screaming, and getting your monologue down pat, is what you say when you instruct.

People have a bad habit of doing whatever it is that you focus their attention on, especially if the command is negative. I had a bit of a time learning this myself even though I had read about the phenomena.

Skilled rock climbers yell "rock" to warn fellow climbers of falling debris. Yelling "heads up" gets your partner smashed in the face with that falling rock you were hollering about. Similarly, if you are teaching a child to ride a bike and they are shakily riding along right towards a tree you don't yell "look out for the tree", you say "steer right (or left)".

Driving is the same. You don't yell to start with; you say "steer left around that bicycle on the shoulder", or "slow down going into the curve". Screaming "look out for the dog" is just about a sure way to turn Rover into road pizza.

12. Don't Feed the Bears

Local law enforcement folks keep us safe and sane in just being visible. If you really want to learn about driving have a long conversation with your local Deputy. But I'll warn you that afterwards you may never let your child drive at all. In my long friendship with a number of Policemen and Deputies, I have come to rely on them as vast source of knowledge about driving and the law in general.

They will tell you things like after midnight they assume the **majority** of drivers on the road are under the influence, they will pull people over who look suspicious in areas known for drug trafficking, they frequently pull people over for driving erratically, and speeding and running red lights are two of the fastest ways to kill yourself or others. They have related stories to me about the people they pull over for DUI eventually coming and thanking them for helping to stop their behavior before they hurt someone else.

I encourage everyone to get to know their local law enforcement folks BEFORE you meet them on the road and they've pulled you over.

Parents, as veteran drivers you (hopefully) know a lot about the area and can give your student a lot of meaningful information while you are driving around town.

Talk to your child about what your expectations are for them on the road, including the possibility that they are stopped by an officer or deputy.

There is no shame in showing your child where the local constabulary frequently set up to catch speeders. One positive thing this does is to make your student aware that the police do, in fact, monitor their speed. Also they set up in lots of places around town so your driver needs to take care about not getting stopped most everywhere.

As you are going around town focusing on speed zones, it's also a good time to remind your student of our list from Chapter 3 – Big Boy/Big Girl rules. They will be upset and you will be upset if they get a ticket, it will be a lot of money and they'll get restricted from driving for a while. Their ticket might also raise your insurance rates. However, they must be polite and professional with the law enforcement person if they get pulled over or the situation may get considerably worse very quickly.

Advice from my friends in law enforcement:

As a father of daughters your protective nature runs really high when those children are teens. There is so much for them to get into danger with and it seems as though there are threats lurking around every corner. I have been fortunate enough to receive frequent counsel, midnight advice, and countless free lessons from my good friends. I pass along the following to you.

- Stay off the roads after midnight if at all possible. It is an extremely hazardous time to be driving and even though you are sober; you may be the only one.

- Stay out of bad neighborhoods, unless you live there. Cars that look like they don't belong in areas known for the trafficking of drugs are routinely pulled over.

- Leave enough space between your car and the car in front of you, enough for you to drive around and or over the curb to get out of a bad situation. Car-jacking, gun fights, incidents of road rage are all realities you deal with on the road.

- Wear your seatbelts. We have a mobile display that travels to our local high schools. This display mimics the experience of a rollover crash. They don't call them crash test dummies for nothing. Those mannequins fly for dozens of yards out the window in that rollover simulator.

- Personally, I've pulled two people out of burning rollover wrecks. Neither had on seat belts and both would have burned up in my absence because they had been beaten senseless as they bounced off their windows on the the inside of their cars.

- Students should never try to work a phone and drive at the same time.

- Alcohol or drugs. I once was sitting in traffic next to a guy as he was lighting and smoking a homemade crack pipe made out of a soda can. Degenerate drug addicts use the same roads you do. One of my Deputy buddies put it best. "We'll catch you, or you'll run into someone or something, and then we'll catch you." Don't take your habit on the road.

- Maintain your car. If your tag light is out and you are driving at night expect to be pulled over. Make sure all of your lights work on the car.

- Slow down. If you think that you are late now, imagine how much later you will be if you get into an accident.

- Don't run the red lights. You will kill people or they will kill you. Both are bad.

- Look around; be aware of your situation and surroundings as before you get to your car in a parking lot. Criminals look for the occupied and clueless because they are easy pickings.

- If you are pulled over by an unmarked car, ask politely to see a badge if the officer is not in uniform and if you are still uncomfortable ask them politely to have a marked car show up.

- Smile and be friendly if you are pulled over. The officers are doing their job, and you are paying them to do it. Warnings are very common, even more so than tickets if everyone is polite.

13. Driven to Distraction

We have covered a lot of ground in the book so far and have discussed how to eliminate driving distractions from our own car.

But what about the other guy on the road? What can we do or should we do when we run into a situation that's liable to include us whether we want it to or not?

Impaired /Erratic Motorists (that are not us)

One of the nice things about the Driver's Education cars the county has provided for us is that they are white, with 9- inch high letters on them that say, **"STUDENT DRIVER"** on both sides and the rear of the car. If we are driving erratically most people have a solid chance at figuring out what's wrong with us. That being said I still came home on a recent Friday after running a class and was grousing to my wife about the *#$%ing morons tailgating us for 2 solid hours in class today. Some people just can't be warned. You can however get out of their way.

Here is an easy discussion we have in class. We get a chance to point this one out about once a week while out driving.

"You see that guy up ahead in the car that's half off the road? Keep an eye on him. See how he's swerving, can't seem to stay in his lane? He's either drunk or texting. As far as you're concerned, there's no difference because he's a danger to you. If he's going slowly enough and the road is clear you can pass him and get beyond him where he's not a danger to you. If he's moving at a high rate of speed, stick back and pay attention because he's liable to wreck someone else who may in turn hit you."

Road Rage

Maybe it's that I'm spending more time on the road and so I get to see more driving behaviors and maybe it's that people are just much more stressed and wrapped up in their own world right now but driving sometimes can be a scary thing.

While we are driving I normally have a discussion with the kids that goes something like this: "You know how lots of people are out of work now and others are worried about their job and their house, etc. The more people become wrapped up in what's going on in their own life, the more distracted they become while out here driving with you. Sometimes you see that as just casual disregard for your safety (or even their own) other times you see it as actual anger at you or others."

Road Rage can look like the guy running up on your bumper (even though you're doing the speed limit) and flashing their lights, or honking (or even waving a fist or a gun). If you run into a case of road rage you need to get away from this person.

Here are some options:

1. Put on your turn signal and pull into the next available driveway or road

2. If on a two lane road and the road is fairly clear, signal to the right, slow and pull slightly over onto the shoulder and allow them to pass.

3. If you pull over and they are still behind you try to get out of their way once more by pulling over

4. If they are still behind you, you should probably find a well-lighted and populated place where you can pull over and get away from this person. Police, fire-station, school., etc. Stopping and calling 911 if you are seriously concerned is also a good idea, so long as the person does not try to attack you while you are stopped.

5. Never, ever under any circumstances confront the person chasing you.

When I took classes for my motorcycle endorsement, I had a really good instructor who counseled us that when dealing with Road Rage you simply can't compete on a motorcycle. Cars too are just safer if you just get out of the irrational person's way. Whatever it was that set this person off, driving in front of them is liable to get you into a car wreck, or worse. It's just not worth your time or energy to deal with the crazies, so don't.

14. The Power of Prayer

People often ask me to repeat myself when I tell them that I run a Driver's Ed class for the county as a part-time job after school.

The incredulous looks and comments about my sanity (not to mention intelligence) are one of the perks of a fairly odd job. I often joke with these same folks that my mother was always after my siblings and I to pray more; so I bought a motorcycle and started teaching Driver's Ed. It worked great, I pray a lot more!

If you want to say a short prayer before going out with your child on the road (or getting on your motorcycle) nobody's going to notice you mumbling to yourself a bit, and if they do, teenagers think you're so old you're feeble-minded anyway so nothing lost there.

15. Deadly Errors

Time to put away the humor for just a moment and deal with a couple serious and extremely common errors new drivers make. As you are doing your driving, please make sure you mention these errors and correct them as quickly as possible. This is serious and lives are at stake.

New Drivers Can't Multitask

As you are teaching a new driver normally they are extremely focused on simply keeping the car inside the travel lane as you are going down the road. Until they have some experience, a new driver cannot steer, check speed, look for people pulling into traffic, see traffic signs, merge or do any of the other myriad things that they need to do simultaneously as an experienced driver.

Not long ago, I had a new driver so focused on keeping the car in the travel lanes that she could not find her way home in her own (really small) neighborhood. She couldn't possibly take her eyes off the road to read the street signs. We were moving at a blistering 15 mph.

Until they are more experienced, please don't ask them to them to do more than one thing at a time. Go slow here, please. You are the instructor and are their eyes and ears. Make sure you do most of their job too.

Black Ice

Black Ice occurs when it has not rained for a time and the roads have accumulated a covering of oil as cars have passed by over time. As soon as it begins to lightly mist rain the oil mixes with the water on the surface of the roads and the road becomes exceptionally slick. Use extra caution at the beginning of a rain with following distance, speed and braking.

No Look Merge

Closely following the previous warning, be extremely careful when asking a student driver to merge. You as the instructor need to make sure the way is clear, before asking a student to merge. Then ask them to put on the proper turn signal, check mirrors and merge when it's clear (even though you know it already is clear). It is a very common rookie mistake for a new driver to be very literal and immediately (and with a jerk) pull into the adjacent lane much to the surprise of the instructor and nearby drivers. Be very careful with your instructions in terms of merging.

Leaving Car Running Before Exiting

As you are doing drills, or switching drivers, especially in the Southern heat, it's is natural to want to leave the car running. It is also common for a driving student not to put the car into park. If you don't want to be run over by your own car, turn the car off every time anyone exits the car. Enough said here.

Pulling into any Intersection without Looking

Just because the light is green doesn't mean it's safe.

I always tell my students that "it doesn't matter if you are in the right if you end up dead". Check both ways, every time, even if you're not the first into the intersection. Point out the really dangerous intersections to your child – they'll thank you later.

To drive this point home I tell all my students the story of bringing home my motorcycle.

I have just purchased my motorcycle and have my bike strapped down in the back of my pickup truck. I come to a stop at the last big intersection on the way home, just about 5 minutes from the house. I'm all excited, ready to unload it and go for a ride after not having ridden for quite a long time.

As I roll up to the intersection, there is a man lying dead in the middle of the intersection, lying next to his motorcycle. The SUV that killed him is parked nearby.

Somebody didn't look, and somebody ran a red light. Doesn't really matter who was at fault to the dead guy.

For some reason I just had to polish that bike a couple days before riding it.

New drivers are focused on staying straight in their lane. Please check those intersections every single time.

Rear-end Collision while Stopped for Traffic

In our area there are a number of high-speed back roads running through rural areas. Most of these roads are two lane roads with speed limits of 55 or 60 which is popularly mandated to mean 65, 70 or higher.

When stopped in traffic it is critical to look in your rear view mirror to see if anyone coming upon your little traffic jam has failed to notice you being stopped. Sometimes you can signal that driver with a turn signal of your own, even though you are not planning to turn, something to make them aware of stopped traffic. Every so often you have to take more direct action to move yourself out of the path of oncoming traffic.

In 3 separate instances I have saved my car, myself and most of my family (this 3rd example was a fatal accident) by pulling out of the travel lanes and allowing the careening car to hit someone else.

You are under no obligation to sit in the road and take a direct hit from an out of control car. Drive off the road

and get out of their way, accelerate and go forward until it is safe, etc.

Big Boy rules can be tough.

Left and Right Errors While Instructing

Note to parents: You would think that after 15 years a young man or woman would know their left from their right.

And you'd be wrong.

This I figured out after a couple exciting trips **off** the road.

When giving instruction from the passenger seat, point and say "I want you to make a left turn" –while pointing to the left, or "I want you to make a right turn" – while pointing to the right. Remember my warning about students not being able to multitask as a new driver. Stressful situations create errors. They are so focused they can't remember their left from their right. Don't put your student in a position to make a serious error. Remember, the life you save may be your own.

Overcorrecting Steering

Perhaps the most common and potentially disastrous error made by new drivers is overcorrecting a steering error. New drivers focus intently on just keeping the car in the travel lane. The newest drivers steer in a jerky, back and forth motion that takes a while to settle out into a smooth, mature steering pattern. Running out of the travel lane (and on two lane roads, off the road) is very common. Since many of the new drivers do not have experience at normal road speeds, they make steering corrections at speed just like they would in a parking lot, hard and jerky.

Jerking the steering wheel to bring the tires back on the road normally sends the car careening off the other direction, requiring a similarly violent correction in the opposite direction. Normally the third of these violent corrections in a row rolls the car over.

My daughter at 18 lost a close friend to this type accident.

It is imperative to teach a new driver how to safely come back into the travel lanes when the car leaves the road. The trick here is to reduce speed, steer straight until you can safely and gently move the wheels back onto the pavement. Please teach your new driver this skill, it's a life saver.

16. Driver's Ed and Students with Disabilities

One of my proudest accomplishments as Driver's Ed instructor was helping students with disabilities learn to drive. In previous classes I have helped students who had physical challenges such as stroke with partial paralysis and a variety of cognitive challenges like Autism, Aspergers syndrome, ADD and ADHD.

The following is my experience and mine alone. It is rendered without legal authority or medical background. You must make good decisions based on your own situation. Your mileage may vary.

If you are the parent of a child with any one of these conditions, I don't have to tell you the challenges you face in everyday life, much less in teaching your child to drive. As the parent, you know what it entails to drive in your community, and you have a really good idea of your child's individual characteristics and maturity level.

As you are starting out to teach your child to drive, depending on your individual situation, it may be helpful for you to teach them and enroll them in classes to allow for extra practice time and work on their skills.

In the end, you as parent make the call as to when your child is allowed to begin the process of licensing. Don't succumb to peer pressure to allow your child to drive at

15 (Florida) if you know they are not ready. Listen to your head as well as the feedback the instructor gives you (if you choose to enroll your child in a class too). As ammunition in the discussion you might need to have with your child, the national average age is rising for students to get their operators permit.

You are the parent, you decide.

In the end my feeling as professional teacher (not professional lawyer or doctor) is in general that you teach your child as much as they will learn about everything you want them to know in this world and be patient if it takes time to learn.

17. Troubleshooting Driving Problems

These are some of the most commonly exhibited problems with rookie drivers. Go ahead and read this section now so you're not even thinking about reading this in the passenger seat as you are instructing.

Remember, you promised you wouldn't.

Burying the car into the turn

One of the most common rookie mistakes is going into the turn with too much speed. Your new driver is so focused on keeping the car in the travel lane that they don't see they're headed into a 15 mph right angle turn at 45 miles per hour. They will figure this out shortly as they slam on the brakes, straighten out the curve and drive off the other side of the road.

You don't have to test this. Believe me it works.

Here's the correction: Your monologue. As you are driving you are quietly saying to the driver, "ok, we're coming up on a turn, slow down into the turn, coast through the turn and now accelerate out of the turn." You know you've said it enough times when they start to repeat it with you and they are actually following your instruction, so 4-500 times should be sufficient.

Jerking the wheel back and forth while driving

It takes a while for your new driver to develop the "touch". Look at their hands on the wheel; are the knuckles white from gripping the wheel too hard? Keep quietly telling them "relax, relax your grip". As they relax a bit they will smooth out their driving.

If that doesn't help try "dampening" the wheel a bit by putting a finger or two on it to make it just a bit harder for them to turn. They'll quickly slow down their turning back and forth.

One other method is to show them (when it's safe) that you can literally run down a straight road without steering at all. Demonstrate (in a safe spot, with your well aligned car) that you don't even need to steer to keep the car moving in a straight line and that by turning the wheel back and forth rapidly they're just making everyone in the car nauseous.

Stopping too late

Correct this error too with your running monologue. As you are coming up on a stop, say "we're coming up to a stop sign, start your stop here, gentle braking". You can stop saying that, just as soon as they start stopping properly.

Weaving in and out of the travel lane

This is one of the most difficult of the rookie errors to correct. It takes infinite patience (you remember that chapter on not yelling right?) and you have to keep repeating over and over and over. Plan on repeating that until that point where you think they may never get it, then they will smooth out and become a good driver. This takes time and practice, and that's just on your part.

As you are going down the road encourage your student to take a distance view of the road. Students tend to look right at the end of the hood and become oblivious to things in the distance. It's kind of like riding a bike; it's easy if you look where you are going. You can drive a straight line with no problem. Now the minute you look down at your feet, your momentum wants to make you fall over.

Driving a car is somewhat similar in that students have to look out ahead a distance and see where the center of the travel lane is located. Once they can see into the distance, steering into the distance seems to resolve most of the back and forth problems that are not related to the hands.

Speed Control

New drivers rarely can tell how fast the car is going. This error you correct as you are correcting the previous one on weaving.

In your monologue you continue saying, "as you are looking down the road and keeping your car in your lane, scan for traffic. Every so often glance down for a half-second to see how fast you are going. Make corrections, continue scanning and checking your speed". Once you feel your tongue begin to detach from your mouth because you've said this so many times, they'll get the habit of driving in their lane and controlling the speed.

Final Notes:

Just in case you haven't picked it up from the reading, the more experience you give your child in the car in terms of hours practiced and varied driving experiences, the faster they will become a competent driver.

There is no substitute for time behind the wheel. Driving cannot be learned from lecture, video games (had that shown to me once) movies or just watching mom or dad drive.

The time you spend with your child in the car can truly be golden time if you would make it so. Once they become competent drivers you have a lot of time to talk about what's going on in their life. So not only are you teaching your child to drive, but you are creating lasting memories that will only make you closer as a family.

Keep bringing 'em in shiny side up!

58589423R00043

Made in the USA
Lexington, KY
14 December 2016